307980

D0571195

First-Aid
Handbook

By Edel Wignell

FALKIRK COUNCIL
LIBRARY SUPPORT
FOR SCHOOLS

Series Literacy Consultant
Dr Ros Fisher

Pearson Education Limited
Edinburgh Gate
Harlow
Essex CM20 2JE
England

www.longman.co.uk

The rights of Edel Wignell to be identified as the author of this Work have been asserted by her in accordance with the Copyright, Designs and Patents Act, 1988.

Text Copyright © 2004 Pearson Education Limited. Compilation Copyright © 2004 Dorling Kindersley Ltd. All rights reserved. No part of this publication may be reproduced, stored in a retrieval system or transmitted in any form or by any means electronic, mechanical, photocopying, recording, or otherwise, without either the prior written permission of the publishers and copyright owners or a licence permitting restricted copying in the United Kingdom issued by the Copyright Licensing Agency Ltd., 90 Tottenham Court Road, London W1P 9HE

ISBN 0 582 84120 8

Colour reproduction by Colourscan, Singapore
Printed and bound in China by Leo Paper Products Ltd.

The Publisher's policy is to use paper manufactured from sustainable forests.

10 9 8 7 6 5 4 3

The following people from **DK** have
contributed to the development of this product:

Art Director Rachael Foster

Martin Wilson **Managing Art Editor**	**Managing Editor** Marie Greenwood
Kath Northam, Ralph Pitchford **Design**	**Editorial** Jennie Morris
Helen McFarland **Picture Research**	**Production** Gordana Simakovic
Richard Czapnik, Andy Smith **Cover Design**	**DTP** David McDonald

Consultants Dr Vivien Armstrong and Richard Walker

Dorling Kindersley would like to thank: Shirley Cachia and Rose Horridge in the DK Picture Library; Andy Crawford for new photography; Johnny Pau for additional cover design work; and models Emel Augustin, Jordan Barber, Nicola Mooi, J.R. Richards Levi and Perry Robinson.

Picture Credits: Alamy Images: Robert Harding World Imagery 26tr. Corbis: Richard Hutchings 6b; Ariel Skelley 7tr; David Stoecklein 7b. Science Photo Library: Faye Norman 30. Topfoto: Ben Graville 12tr.

All other images: Dorling Kindersley © 2004. For further information see www.dkimages.com
Dorling Kindersley Ltd., 80 Strand, London WC2R 0RL

Contents

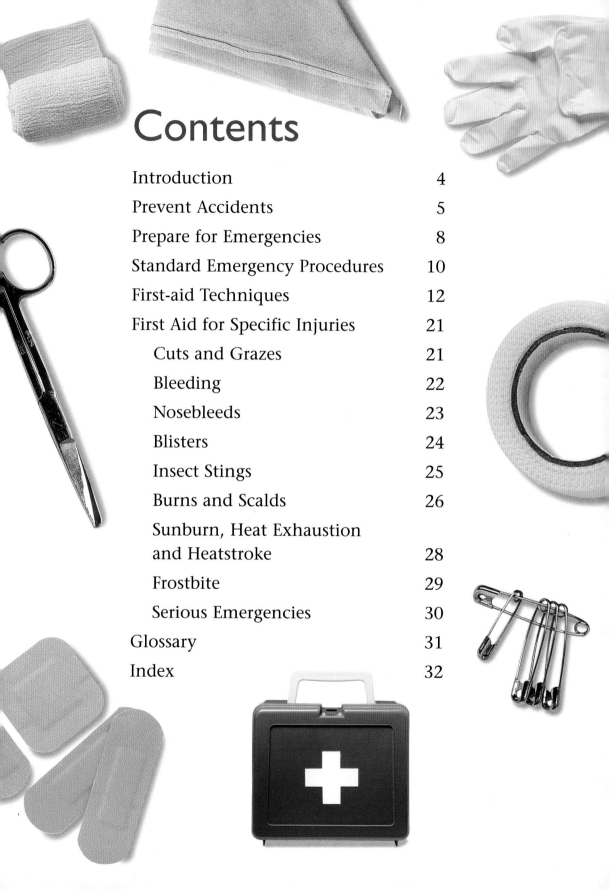

Introduction	4
Prevent Accidents	5
Prepare for Emergencies	8
Standard Emergency Procedures	10
First-aid Techniques	12
First Aid for Specific Injuries	21
Cuts and Grazes	21
Bleeding	22
Nosebleeds	23
Blisters	24
Insect Stings	25
Burns and Scalds	26
Sunburn, Heat Exhaustion and Heatstroke	28
Frostbite	29
Serious Emergencies	30
Glossary	31
Index	32

Introduction

What should you do if you cut your leg or your nose starts to bleed? What if your friend has a blister or is stung by a bee?

If you know what to do in the case of an emergency, you can save lives. That's why it's important to take a first-aid class. In the meantime, this book will help you plan for emergencies. It will guide you through some first-aid procedures to help you deal with accidents. It will also show you how to prevent them.

Some injuries are easy to treat.

Prevent Accidents

Most injuries are caused by accidents, and many accidents can be prevented. Just as good health practices can help to prevent illness, good safety practices can help to prevent accidents. Use the following tips to stay safe in different situations.

Have smoke detectors installed at home.

Home Safety

Follow these tips to make your home safe:

- Be careful where you play. Stairs, landing areas and bunk beds can be dangerous places.
- Keep toys and clutter away from stairs and other areas where they could trip people.
- Use a rubber mat that grips to keep from slipping in the bath or shower.
- Be careful with boiling water and hot drinks. These are the most common causes of burns and scalds in the home.
- Make sure you have smoke detectors with working batteries. Test them regularly. Make sure everyone in your
- home knows what to do in case of a fire. Work out how you would leave the building and practise your escape plan.

Travel Safety

Take care when you are travelling by car, cycling or walking. Always wear a seat belt in a car, and remember the following tips when cycling or walking.

helmet

Cycling

- Make sure your bike is in good working order.
- Always wear a helmet and follow all safety rules and traffic signals.
- Be on your guard when crossing the road. It is hard to judge the speed of approaching traffic.
- Wear bright or fluorescent clothing so drivers will see you.

Walking

- Follow traffic laws, and pay attention to signs and signals.
- Never cross the road between two parked cars – always cross at crossings.
- Never chase a ball, a friend or a pet into the road.

Lollipop men and ladies help you cross roads safely.

Sports Safety

To stay safe while playing sports, follow these tips:

- Wear the protective equipment necessary for each sport you play. For example, wear a helmet to prevent serious head injuries.
- Always swim with a partner, and make sure an adult is watching you.
- Never play or skateboard near a road at night or at dusk. Drivers can't see you well. You should not cycle at night for the same reason, even with lights and reflectors.

Wear the proper safety equipment for your sport.

helmet with visor

padded gloves

knee pads

Prepare for Emergencies

Accidents happen – but if you are prepared for emergencies, it is easier to stay calm and do what is necessary. Here are some things you can do to prepare for a medical emergency.

Make a list of emergency telephone numbers in your area. This should include police, fire, ambulance and poison control. Highlight the number that would get you help the fastest. This number is usually 999. Place a copy of the list by each phone in your home.

Making an Emergency Call

When you make an emergency call, you may be asked for the following information:

- your telephone number
- exactly where the emergency is
- what the emergency is
- how serious the emergency is
- who is involved and basic information about the person, including age, sex and condition.

Stay on the line when you make an emergency call. This is especially important if you don't know the exact address of the accident so that emergency services can trace your call.

Put together a first-aid kit with the help of an adult. It should include the items in the list to the right. Make sure that the bandages and gauze pads are **sterile**.

First-aid Kit Checklist

✔ a well-marked, waterproof box
✔ disposable gloves
✔ plasters
✔ roller bandages
✔ adhesive tape
✔ gauze pads
✔ antiseptic wipes
✔ torch
✔ cold compress
✔ tweezers
✔ large triangular bandage
✔ safety pins
✔ scissors

First-aid Kit

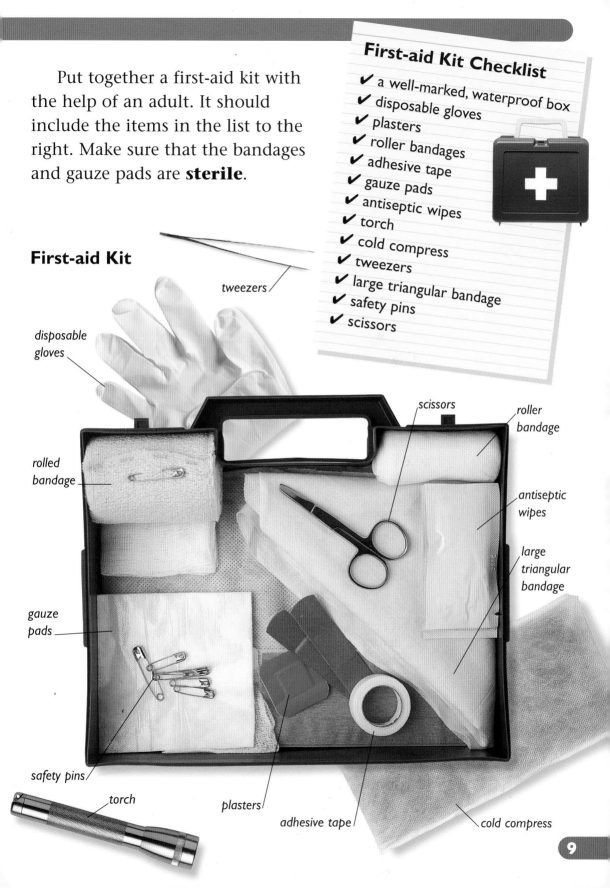

tweezers

disposable gloves

scissors

roller bandage

rolled bandage

antiseptic wipes

large triangular bandage

gauze pads

safety pins

torch

plasters

adhesive tape

cold compress

Standard Emergency Procedures

In the case of an emergency, here are steps you should follow:

1 Try to stay calm. Take enough time to think clearly.

2 Look around and work out what has happened. Make sure you are safe.

3 Get help by finding an adult and a telephone. Phone the emergency number and be ready to answer the emergency service's questions.

4 Do what you can for an injured person. Remember, you need training to give first aid for many injuries, but even without training you can still help.

Help the injured person feel at ease.

5 Do what you can to make sure the injured person is calm. Talk to the injured person, and let him or her know help is on the way. Don't let him or her move. Don't give him or her anything to eat or drink. Watch the injured person carefully so you will be able to provide important information when help arrives.

Dealing With People in Shock

In an emergency, the injured person may be in shock. Shock is the body's reaction to loss of blood, a severe burn or another injury or illness. Symptoms, or signs, include feeling faint or dizzy, fast and shallow breathing and pale, cold and sweaty skin. Shock is life-threatening. If you think the injured person is in shock, then help him or her to lie down and raise his or her legs above heart level, supporting them with pillows or cushions. Keep the person warm, comfortable and calm. Then call for help immediately.

First-aid Techniques

A good way to be prepared for an emergency that requires first-aid assistance is to take a class. Many organizations offer first-aid classes that teach how to help save lives. Before you are fully trained, you can practise some of the first-aid techniques used in emergencies.

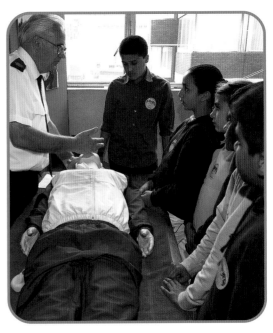

In first-aid classes, special equipment helps students learn emergency techniques.

What Is a Pulse?

A **pulse** is the rate at which the heart beats. It provides important health information. Any change in a normal pulse rate can signal danger. In an emergency, you may need to take a pulse. You can feel the pulse at the wrist, neck or upper arm.

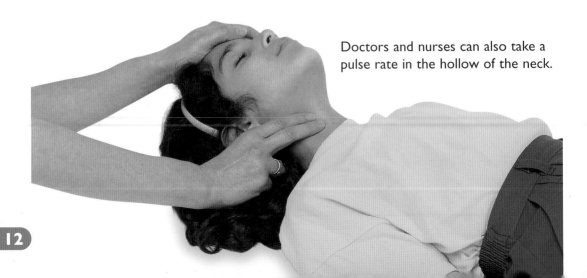

Doctors and nurses can also take a pulse rate in the hollow of the neck.

Taking a Pulse

This is how to take your pulse rate at your wrist:

1 Find a watch that measures seconds, and place it where you can see it.

2 There is a spot on your wrist, just below the base of the thumb, where it is easiest to find your pulse. Put the index and middle finger of one hand on that spot on the wrist of your other hand.

3 To determine the pulse rate, feel the pulse point for 10 seconds, counting the number of pulses you feel. Then multiply this number by 6.

Pulse Rates

Pulse rates change depending on age, exercise and stress. Exercise such as skipping increases pulse rates.

Circulatory System

A drop in blood flow is often caused by changes in circulation (the movement of blood through the body). In the body's circulatory system, the heart muscle forces blood through the arteries. The arteries are a network of blood vessels. Blood returns to the heart through blood vessels called veins. Tiny capillaries connect the arteries and veins. The capillaries take oxygen to all the cells, or basic units of the human body. They also remove waste from the cells.

Unconscious People

Someone who is **unconscious** is unaware of what is going on around him or her. A person might become unconscious from bleeding, fainting, **heat exhaustion**, a heart attack, a head or spinal injury, diabetes or other injuries or illnesses. Fainting is caused by a temporary drop in blood flow to the brain that leads to unconsciousness.

Putting Someone in the Recovery Position

A person who is **semi-conscious** or unconscious should be put in the recovery position. This position makes it easier for the injured person to breathe. If the person has a back, leg or neck injury then try not to move him or her into the recovery position unless he or she is having trouble breathing or is vomiting. In that case, it may be necessary to move the person into the recovery position carefully.

Practise these steps with a partner:

I Straighten the person's legs. Place the arm that is nearer to you at a right angle to the body.

2 Place the other arm across the chest. Put the back of this hand against the opposite cheek.

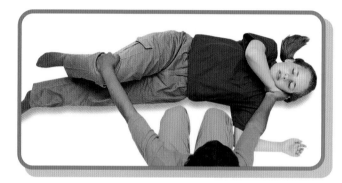

3 Lift the leg that is furthest from you. Pull the knee up and bend the leg until the foot is flat on the ground.

4 Roll the person onto his or her side, with the hand still by the cheek.

5 Bend the top leg into a right angle and adjust the arm to prevent the person from rolling forwards. Gently tilt the head back and lift the chin forwards to keep the air passages open.

Putting on a Roller Bandage

Bandages protect wounds, stop bleeding, support injured joints and hold dressings in place. To work best, the width of the bandages should be about the same as the injured part of the body. It takes practice to put on bandages. If the bandages are put on too tightly, then they can seriously damage the wounded area. If they aren't put on tightly enough, then they might not stop the bleeding.

Roller bandages come in various sizes.

To practise bandaging, follow these steps:

1 Support the injured body part. Hold the roller bandage in one hand, with the loose end coming off the top. Put the end of the bandage below the injury and wrap around twice.

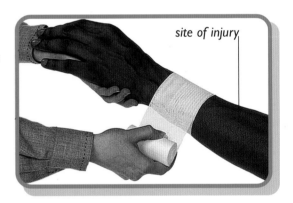

site of injury

2 Check to make sure you aren't wrapping too tightly. Leave the tips of fingers or toes unwrapped. If they start tingling, get numb or cold, or change colour, then the bandage is too tight. Loosen it immediately.

Press and release nail to check circulation. The pink colour under the nail should return quickly.

3 Continue to wrap the bandage around the limb, overlapping at least half of the previous layer. Do not pull or stretch the bandage as it unrolls. This will make it too tight.

4 Secure the bandage, using adhesive tape or safety pins, or by tucking in the ends. Check the tightness again as explained in Step 2.

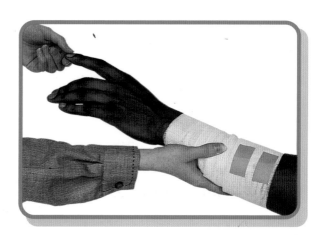

Securing Roller Bandages

There are several ways to secure roller bandages.

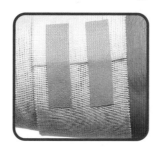

| safety pin | adhesive tape | tucking in the ends |

Using Triangular Bandages

Triangular bandages can be used as dressings to protect wounds or to stop bleeding. They can also be used as head bandages and as slings. Slings help support injured arms.

Practise making an arm sling with a friend:

1 Support the injured arm against the chest. Put one end of the sling over the shoulder opposite the injured arm and spread the sling out across the chest and under the injured arm. Put the point of the triangle under the elbow.

2 Bring the lower end of the sling up over the injured arm to the other shoulder. Tie the two ends of the sling together on the side of the neck. Make a reef knot, following the steps on the next page.

3 Tuck in any loose ends of the sling at the elbow. Secure the sling with a safety pin. Make sure you can see the fingers. Check to make sure it isn't too tight.

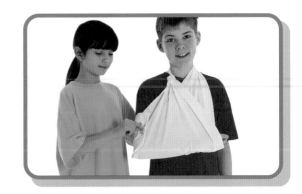

In an emergency, first-aid equipment isn't always available. Try making a sling using a jumper or a jacket. The arm can be supported by the body of the jumper and tied firmly on the shoulder, using the arms of the jumper as ties.

Tying a Reef Knot

A reef knot won't slip and can be easily untied when necessary. This is how to tie a reef knot:

1 Cross the left end (yellow) over the right end (blue).

2 Take the yellow end under and through.

3 Pass the yellow end over the blue end and through the hole.

4 Pull the ends to tighten.

Bandaging Joints

Roller bandages also support injured ankles and wrists if put on in a figure-of-eight pattern.

Follow these steps:

1 Start with the end of the bandage and wrap it around the joint twice.

2 Place the bandage diagonally above the joint and wrap it around. Then place the bandage diagonally below the joint and wrap it around. Make sure it is not too tight.

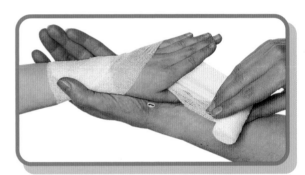

3 Continue winding the bandage in this figure-of-eight pattern, each time covering at least half of the previous layer. Leave the tips of fingers or toes uncovered.

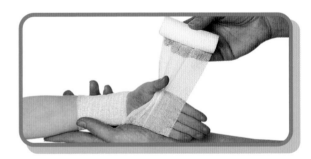

4 End with two straight wraps. Secure the bandage with adhesive tape or safety pins. Check to make sure it isn't too tight.

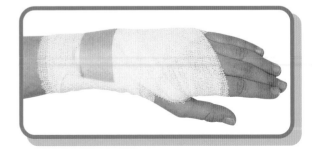

First Aid for Specific Injuries

Cuts and Grazes

If you have a minor cut or graze, then follow the steps below. Most cuts usually stop bleeding on their own or with some direct pressure.

Wash your hands well to prevent infection, and remember never to touch another person's cuts or blood. Always wear disposable gloves when treating somone else.

1 Wash the wound very gently with a gauze pad and warm, clean water. Make sure you remove all dirt, as it could carry harmful **bacteria**, or germs that might cause infection in the wound. Then pat the clean wound dry.

2 Press a clean gauze pad down on the wound to stop the bleeding. Press it firmly for a minute or two.

3 Dress the wound with a plaster or piece of gauze large enough to cover the wound and the area around it. If you use gauze, then secure it with adhesive tape.

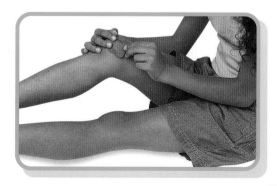

Bleeding

Here's what to do if you have a more severe cut:

Ask someone nearby to help you. If possible, call an emergency number.

1 Stop the bleeding by pressing a clean gauze pad or cloth over the wound. If you can't find any cloth, use your hand. Keep pressing until the bleeding stops. This can take 10 minutes.

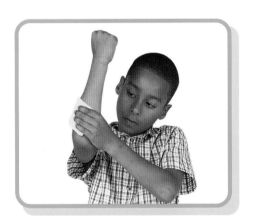

2 If possible, raise the injured part of your body and keep it above the level of your heart. This will keep the blood flow away from the injured area.

3 Lie down. Keep the injured part high and your head low. This will help reduce shock. Keep pressure on the wound until the bleeding has stopped. If you can, get someone to help you cover the wound with a **sterile** dressing or pad that is larger than the wound. Tie a bandage firmly around the dressing.

Nosebleeds

If your nose bleeds, then follow these steps, and the nosebleed should stop.

1 Sit down and put your head forwards. Breathe through your mouth. Firmly pinch your nostrils together for 5 to 10 minutes. Direct pressure should stop the nosebleed.

2 If blood runs into your mouth, spit it into a tissue. Wait for 10 minutes. If the bleeding hasn't stopped, pinch the nostrils again for another 10 minutes, then for 10 more. Be patient! Don't expect it to stop too quickly.

3 When the bleeding stops, clean around your nose and mouth with a flannel dipped in lukewarm water. Rest for a few minutes to give the inside of your nose time to heal. Don't blow your nose.

Blisters

Anything that rubs the skin too much can cause a friction blister. Blisters form on the top layer of skin (**epidermis**). Although blisters can be painful, they form to protect the tissue underneath. If the blister is closed, then leave it alone.

This is how to treat an open blister:

1 Clean the blister with soap and water. Rinse it with clean water. Keep the flap of skin, unless it looks dirty. Smooth it gently over the skin beneath.

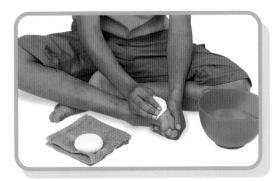

2 Put on an adhesive bandage to prevent infection.

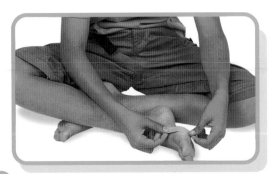

Skin

Your skin is made up of two layers: the epidermis and the **dermis**. Receptors in your skin make sure that your body is sensitive to heat, cold, pain and touch. Blisters form when the connection between the two layers is broken.

Structure of the Skin

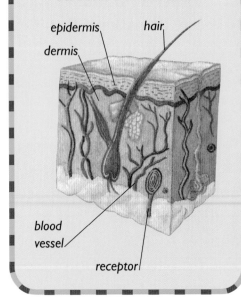

epidermis   hair

dermis

blood vessel

receptor

Insect Stings

When you are stung by an insect such as a bee or wasp, this is the best way to treat the sting:

1 If the sting is still in your skin, then brush or scrape it off sideways with your fingernail. Do not use tweezers because more poison may be squeezed into the wound.

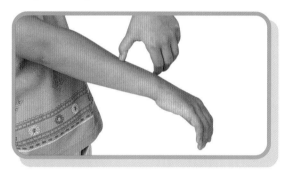

2 Cool the area with a cold compress for about 10 minutes. This can be an ice pack or a cold, damp cloth. This will ease the pain of the sting.

Insect Bite Allergies

Some people are allergic to bee and wasp stings. If they get stung, then they can become dizzy, get hives (red, raised patches on their skin), have difficulty breathing or have a swollen tongue and face. If you see someone having this kind of reaction, then get help immediately.

If you have had a serious allergic reaction in the past, then you should always carry an emergency allergy kit. This kit contains auto-injectors, which are special syringes that have a single dose of medication built into them. This medication will stop or help to lessen the allergic reaction.

auto-injector

Treating an allergic reaction with an auto-injector.

Burns and Scalds

Burns are common injuries. Besides being painful, burned skin cannot act as a barrier against infection.

Burns are labelled by degree. A first-degree burn damages only the top layer of your skin, the **epidermis**. Your skin becomes red, swollen and tender, like a mild sunburn. It can usually be treated at home.

A second-degree burn damages several layers of skin. Your skin becomes red and raw. Fluid is released from the damaged tissues, and blisters form on your skin. This should be treated by a doctor.

A third-degree burn damages all the layers of your skin, as well as nerves, fat tissue, muscles and blood vessels. This burn needs urgent hospital attention.

kettle

iron

Burns from heat or steam are common.

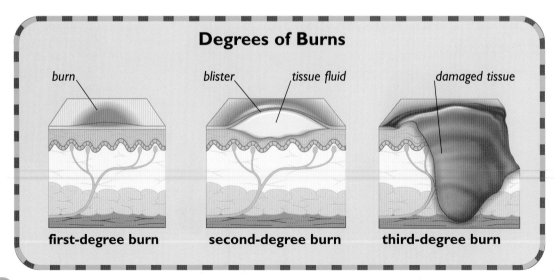

Degrees of Burns

burn

blister   tissue fluid

damaged tissue

first-degree burn   **second-degree burn**   **third-degree burn**

If you have a small first-degree burn, you can usually treat it by following these steps:

1 First hold the injured part under cold running water or on a cold pack for 10 minutes.

2 Protect the burn by covering it with a clean plastic bag or bandage. Change it after 24 hours. Never put butter on a burn. You should not put ointment on a burn unless told to by a medical professional.

(!) If a blister forms, don't break it. If you do, you may introduce infection into the wound. A blister may also signal a second-degree burn that needs to be seen by a doctor.

There are many things around the home that you can use to protect a burn.

pillowcase

tea towel

cling film

Sunburn

Most sunburn is a first-degree burn. Sunburned skin is red, itchy and sore. If you get sunburn, go into the shade or a cool room, and sip cool drinks. Spread aftersun lotion on sunburned skin.

Aftersun lotion soothes sunburned skin.

Heat Exhaustion

If your body can't cool itself through sweating, then you can get heat exhaustion. This gives you a headache, makes you feel dizzy and you may vomit. Your skin is clammy and pale, too.

This is how to treat heat exhaustion:

1 Lie down in a cool place with pillows under your legs. This will send blood to your brain. Rest for an hour or two.

2 You may also be **dehydrated**, or lack enough water in your body. Sip cool drinks until you feel better.

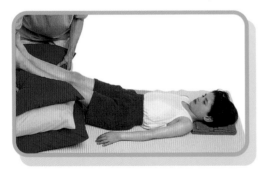

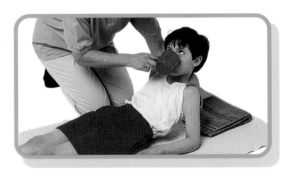

Heatstroke

You can get **heatstroke** when your body fails to cool itself and your temperature rises. Heatstroke is very serious. Emergency medical care is always needed.

Frostbite

If you spend time outdoors in freezing weather, then your fingers, toes and nose may get **frostbite**. This is when your skin or underlying tissues are frozen. There are different levels of frostbite. If your hands or feet have mild frostbite, then your skin will feel tingly or slightly numb and will look white.

Dangerous Frostbite

If you have a more serious form of frostbite, then your skin will be white, blotchy or blue. It will feel hard and very cold. See a doctor immediately.

This is how to treat frostbite:

1 Go into a warm room and carefully take off any tight things such as your gloves, shoes, socks and rings. Warm your hands by placing them under your armpits. Thaw your feet by putting them inside warm blankets or next to your skin.

2 Put the frostbitten body part in warm (not hot) water for 15 to 30 minutes. Do *not* rub your feet or hands or use a hot-water bottle or a radiator to warm your feet or hands.

Hypothermia

A condition called **hypothermia** results when your body loses heat faster than it can produce it. Hypothermia can happen in any season when a person is exposed to cold rain or submerged in cold water. It can be serious, leading to unconsciousness or death.

Serious Emergencies

There are many first-aid procedures you can follow with more training. Young people have saved others from choking by using the **Heimlich manoeuvre**. They have stopped severe bleeding, and they have helped people with serious allergic reactions.

If you are interested in first aid, then you can read more books or take a first-aid class. With knowledge and experience, you can use first-aid procedures to help take care of injured people until medical help arrives. You may also be able to help yourself in emergency situations.

Some first-aid procedures, such as the Heimlich manoeuvre, should be learned from a first-aid professional.

Glossary

bacteria	organisms that can cause diseases or infection; some bacteria are harmless, while others are harmful
dehydrated	not enough water in the body
dermis	lower layer of the skin
epidermis	upper layer of the skin
frostbite	when parts of the body become frozen
heat exhaustion	when heavy sweating leads to loss of fluids and salts
heatstroke	a medical emergency that happens when the body's cooling system stops working
Heimlich manoeuvre	a first-aid procedure used to help someone who is choking
hypothermia	when the body temperature falls below normal and cannot be increased
pulse	heartbeat that can be felt at the throat, wrist or upper arm
semi-conscious	when someone is only partly aware of his or her surroundings
sterile	free of germs
unconscious	when someone is completely unaware of his or her surroundings

Index

allergy 25, 30

bacteria 21

bandages 9, 16–17, 18, 20

bleeding 4, 14, 16, 18, 21, 22, 23, 30

blister 4, 24, 26, 27

breathing 11, 14, 25

burns 5, 11, 26–27, 28

choking 30

circulation 14, 16

cuts 4, 21, 22

emergency procedures 8, 10–11

fainting 11, 14

first-aid kit 9

frostbite 29

heat exhaustion 14, 28

heatstroke 28

hypothermia 29

infection 21, 26, 27

insect stings 4, 25

nosebleeds 4, 23

pulse 12–13

recovery position 14–15

safety 5, 6–7

scalds 5, 26

shock 11, 22

skin 11, 24–25, 26–27, 28–29

sunburn 26, 28